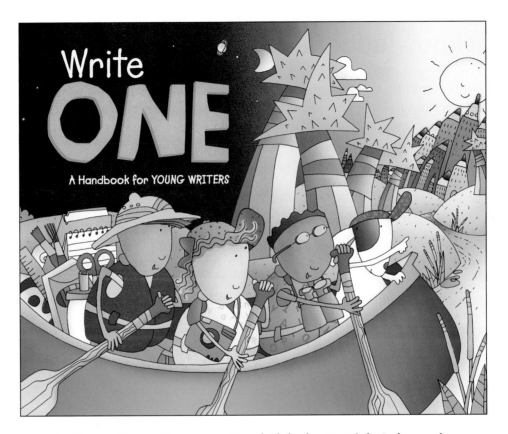

Write
ONE
A Handbook for YOUNG WRITERS

Authors **Dave Kemper, Carol Elsholz, Patrick Sebranek**
Illustrator **Chris Krenzke**

WRITE SOURCE®

GREAT SOURCE EDUCATION GROUP
a Houghton Mifflin Company
Wilmington, Massachusetts

Acknowledgements

We're grateful to many people who helped bring *Write One* to life. First, we must thank all the students from across the country who contributed their writing models and ideas. Also, thanks to the writers, editors, and teachers who helped make this book a reality.

Betsey Bystol   Jim MacCall
Nancy Koceja   Deb Pingle
Dian Lynch   Pat Reigel

In addition, we want to thank our Write Source/Great Source team for all their help: Laura Bachman, Colleen Belmont, Sherry Gordon, Lois Krenzke, Ellen Leitheusser, Sue Paro, and Sandy Wagner.

Write One You'll Have Fun!

The Process of Writing This part tells you all about being a writer.

The Forms of Writing Here you'll learn about writing notes, stories, poems, and more.

Tools of Learning In this part you'll learn about listening, speaking, and reading and writing new words.

Proofreader's Guide In this part you'll find out how to use capital letters and punctuation.

Student Almanac This part has maps, math charts, pictures, names of animals and places, and lots more.

Table of Contents

The **Process** of Writing

All About Writing

12 Jenny Writes

22 Traits of Good Writing

24 Steps in the Writing Process

    24 Plan

    25 Write

    26 Revise

    26 Check

    27 Publish

The Forms of Writing

Personal Writing

30 Writing in Journals
32 Writing Lists
34 Writing Friendly Notes
36 Writing E-Mail Messages
38 Writing Friendly Letters
40 Writing Stories About Me

Subject Writing

44 Writing About Others
46 Writing a Description
48 How-To Writing
50 Writing Captions
52 Making Alphabet Books
54 Writing About Books

Research Writing

58 Writing Reports
62 Writing in Learning Logs

Story and Poetry Writing

66 Writing Stories
68 Writing Poems
72 Writing with Patterns

The **Process** of Writing
The **Forms** of Writing
The **Tools** of Learning
Proofreader's Guide
Student Almanac

6

The Tools of Learning

Listening and Speaking Skills

76 Listening to Others
78 Speaking to Others
80 Working Together

Reading and Word-Study Skills

84 Reading to Understand
86 Reading New Words
  88 Consonant Blends
  89 Consonant Digraphs
  90 Long Vowels
  91 Short Vowels
  92 Rhyming Families
  94 Contractions
  95 Compound Words
96 Using Alphabet Lists

Proofreader's Guide

Rules for Writing

126 Writing Sentences

128 Using Capital Letters

129 Making Plurals

130 Using Punctuation

134 Understanding Our Language

136 Using Everyday Words

140 Using the Right Word

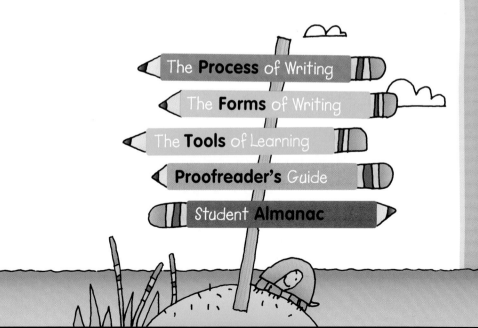

The **Process** of Writing

The **Forms** of Writing

The **Tools** of Learning

Proofreader's Guide

Student **Almanac**

Student **Almanac**

Lists, Maps, and Theme Words

148 Practicing Handwriting

    150 Manuscript Models

    152 Continuous Stroke Models

154 Using a Computer

156 Using Maps

    157 World Map

    158 North America Map

    159 United States Map

160 Working with Math

    161 Telling Time

    162 Numbers 1 to 100

    163 Place Value

    164 Bar Graphs

    165 Money

    166 Addition and Subtraction

    167 Fractions

168 Using Theme Words

169 Days of the Week

170 Months of the Year

172 Seasons and Weather

174 Numbers and Colors

176 Places

178 Parks

180 Plants

182 Food Pyramid

184 Animals of the . . .

186 Five Senses

188 Index

All About Writing

In this part of your handbook, you will meet Jenny, Luke, Rosa, and Ben. They are writers. You can be a writer, too.

Jenny Writes

It's writing time in Room 101. Luke is planning a story. Rosa is writing a poem. Ben is writing something silly.

Jenny wonders, "What can I write?"

Jenny asks Luke what he's writing. Luke tells her he's writing a dog story. It's about his three dogs. Luke knows a lot about dogs.

Jenny still wonders, "What can I write?"

Jenny asks Rosa about her poem.
Rosa reads it to Jenny. It's about
the time she went fishing with her
grandpa. Rosa's poem rhymes.

How we wish
we had a fish.

fish

Jenny still wonders, "What can I write?"

Then Ben pops up next to Jenny's desk. Ben shows her the silly note he wrote. Jenny and Ben laugh at the note.

Suddenly Jenny thinks, "This note gives me an idea."

Just like her friends, Jenny begins to write and draw.

Jenny writes a note to her mom and dad.

Hi Mom and Dad,
I like cats.
Luke has three
BIG DOGS!
I wish we had
one little cat.

Love,
Jenny

A
B
C
D
E
F
G
H
I
J
K
L
M
N
O
P
Q
R
S
T
U
V
W
X
Y
Z

Traits of Good Writing

Good writing has these special things:

Interesting Ideas

Write about things that interest you.

Clear Order

Plan a beginning, a middle, and an ending.

Well-Chosen Words

Find the right words to say what you mean.

Personal Voice

Make your writing sound like you.

Smooth Sentences

Write sentences that are easy to read out loud.

Correct Copy

Find ways to spell words. Get help with your punctuation, too.

Steps in the Writing Process

The **writing process** has five steps: plan, write, revise, check, and publish.

1

PLAN

- Talk.
- Draw.
- Think.
- Write lists.

Things Pets Need

1. food
2. water
3. love
4. a plas to sleep
5. toys

2

WRITE

- Write sentences about the topic.
- Spell words the best you can.
- Use your plan as you write.

SPOT

Things Pets Need

Pets need food and water. Pets like to be loved. they need a plas to sleep. Pets like to have toys.

A
C
D E
F
G
I J
K
L
M N
O
P
S R
S
T
U V
X W
Z Y
Z

3

REVISE

- Read it aloud.
- Does it sound right?
- Make changes.

4

CHECK

- Capitals
- Punctuation
- Spelling

Things Pets Need

Pets need food and ∧ *fresh*

water. Pets like to be

loved. <u>T</u>they need a ~~plas~~ *place*

to sleep. Pets like to have

fun
to~~y~~s.

5

PUBLISH

- Make a neat copy.
- Share it with others.
- Put it in a class book.

Things Pets Need

Pets need food and fresh water. Pets like to be loved. They need a place to sleep. Pets like to have fun.

by Krista

The **Forms** of Writing

Personal Writing

Your life is full of ideas you can share. Write about these ideas in stories, letters, and journals.

Writing in Journals

A **journal** is your very own place for writing. You can write in your journal every day.

- Write the date.

- Draw a picture if you want to.

- Write about things you do and think about.

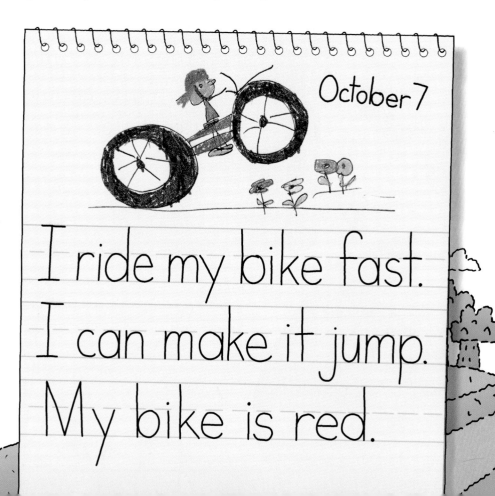

October 7

I ride my bike fast.
I can make it jump.
My bike is red.

A journal is waiting for your words.

Ideas for your journal:

▸ A story about a friend

▸ A wish list

▸ Something you like to do

▸ Places you like to go

▸ Poems

▸ Questions you want to ask

▸ A list of books you've read

▸ Jokes

Writing Lists

Lists are easy to write. They can be long or short, serious or silly. You can write lists for many reasons.

Show what you know.

Wild Animals
lion
deer
snake
wolf
ape
hippo

Have fun.

Remember things.

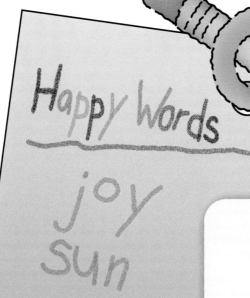

Happy words

joy
sun
smile
jump

Store

corn
milk
apples
peanut butter

More list ideas:

▶ Favorite things
▶ Pets
▶ Games
▶ Words
▶ Friends
▶ Things to do
▶ Colors

Writing Friendly Notes

Writing a **friendly note** is fun. Your note can be an invitation, a reply, or a thank-you.

An Invitation

Lea,
You are funny.
Do you want to
play at my house?
Say YES.
Michelle

A Reply

Dear Michelle,
I can come
to your house.
Tell your mom
to call my mom.
Lea

A Thank-You Note

Hi Michelle,

I had fun at your house. Thanks for the ladybug pin.

Lea

Other note ideas:

- Facts about things
- Kind things
- Funny things

Writing E-Mail Messages

You can write an **e-mail message** without using paper or pencil. You write it on a computer, using a keyboard.

There are four important parts to e-mail:

1 From:
(Your address will appear here.)

2 To:
(Type the address you are sending to.)

3 Subject:
(Type what your message is about.)

4 Message:
(Type your message here.)

From: pmartin@pflora.net

To: mlopez@pflora.net

Cc:

Subject: Long Lake

Attach:

Dear Uncle Marco,

We are going to Long Lake next week.
Can you come camping with us?
We'll have LOTS of fun!

Love,
Paco

Writing Friendly Letters

You can write a **friendly letter** to someone near or faraway.

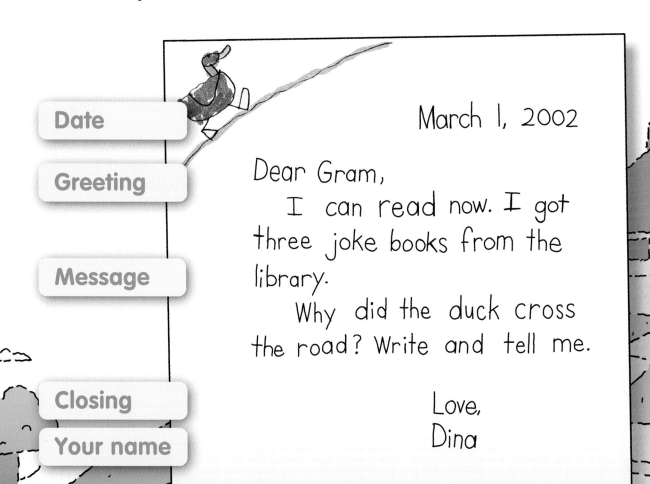

Date

Greeting

Message

Closing

Your name

March 1, 2002

Dear Gram,
    I can read now. I got three joke books from the library.
    Why did the duck cross the road? Write and tell me.

Love,
Dina

Sending Your Letter

Address the envelope. Add a stamp.
Then send your letter.

DINA BENJAMIN
440 OAK ST
DENVER CO 80202

Your address

MRS JUDITH MURPHY
86 PARK AVE
RICHMOND VA 23201

Mailing address

Writing Stories About Me

A **story about me** is about a special time in your life. A cluster can help you plan your story.

Make a cluster.

Jesse

Josh came home.

I held him.

A Happy Day

He didn't cry.

He was in a yellow blanket.

Write a story from the cluster.

A Happy Day

One day baby Josh came home.
He was in a yellow blanket. My
mom let me hold him. He was
blowing bubbles. He didn't cry.

by Jesse

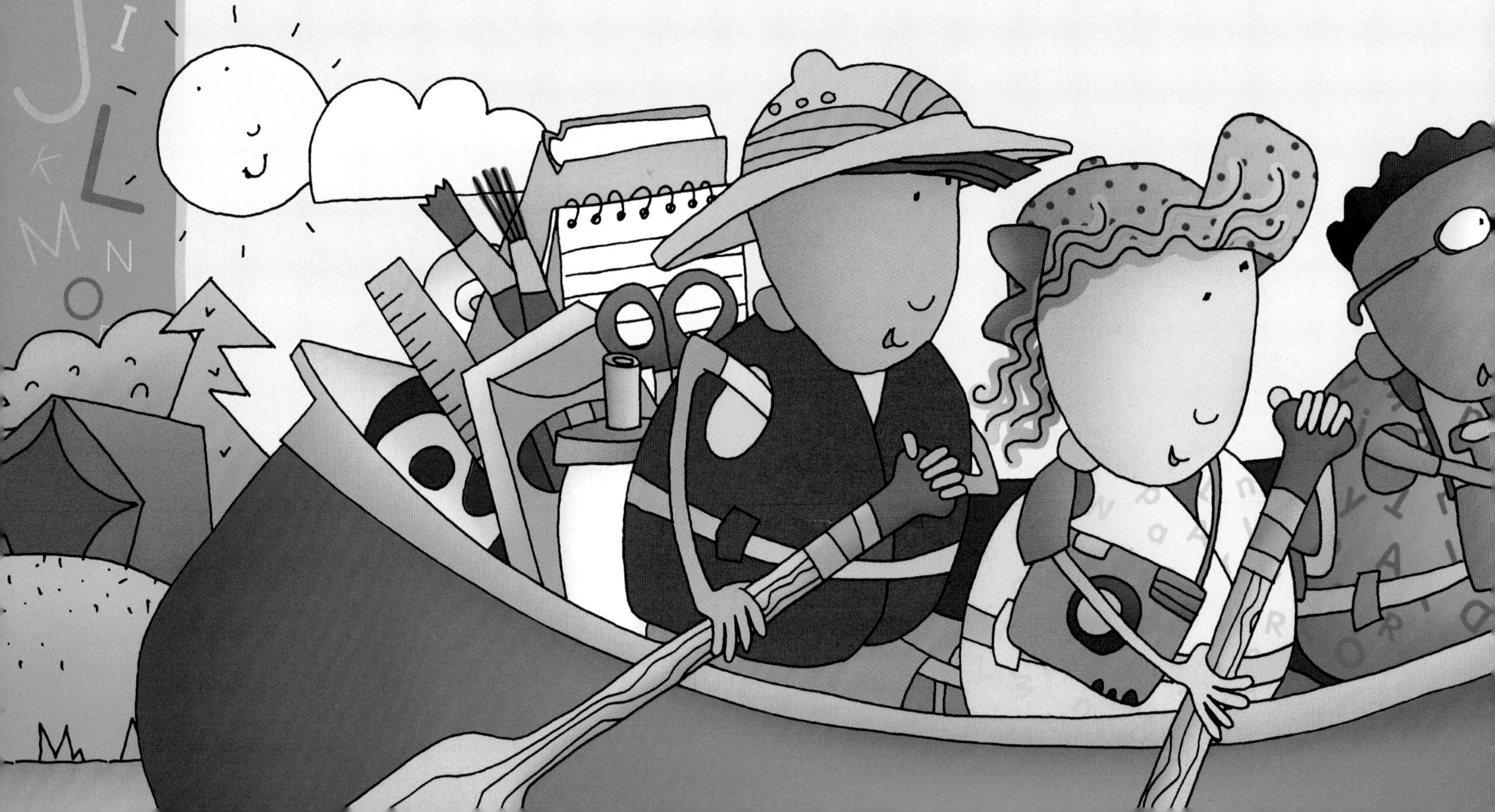

Subject Writing

It's fun to talk about interesting people, places, and things. You can write about them, too.

BACDEFGHIJKLMNOPQRSTUVWXYZ

Writing About Others

Do you know someone you can write about?
Start with an important idea about this person.
Then write details that tell about your idea.

Important idea

Details

Silly Nick

My cousin Nick is silly. He puts
potato chips in his soup. He wears
two different socks. Sometimes he
wears a bow tie. When he sleeps
over at my house, he brings his
goldfish along.

by Timothy

People to write about:

▶ A special friend

▶ A relative

▶ Your funny neighbor

▶ A famous person

▶ Your baby-sitter

Writing a Description

You can write **descriptions** about people, places, or things.

- Tell how something **LOOKS**.

- Tell how something **FEELS**.

Our New Car

Our new car is green.
It has a sunroof.
It has soft tan seats.
It is sporty.
My dad thinks it's cool.

Use Your Senses

Pick words that give details.

My Grandma

My grandma sings a lot. She smells like peppermints.

- Tell how someone **SOUNDS**.

- Tell how someone **SMELLS**.

A B C D E F G H I J K L M N O P Q R S T U V W X Y Z

How-To Writing

When you write **directions**, you tell how to do something. Use *words* or *numbers* to put the steps in order.

Start with words.

Making Chocolate Milk

First, pour some milk in a glass.

Next, put 2 spoons of chocolate syrup in.

Then, stir it for 1 minute.

Last, drink it. Yum!

by Michael

Start with numbers.

Getting Ready for School
by Betsey

1. Wash up and get dressed.
2. Eat breakfast.
3. Brush your teeth.
4. Grab your schoolbag and go.

Other directions:

▶ Taking care of a pet
▶ Making breakfast
▶ Making a friend

Writing Captions

Adding **captions** to pictures makes them more interesting. Captions give you special information.

We love reading time.

Journals go everywhere!

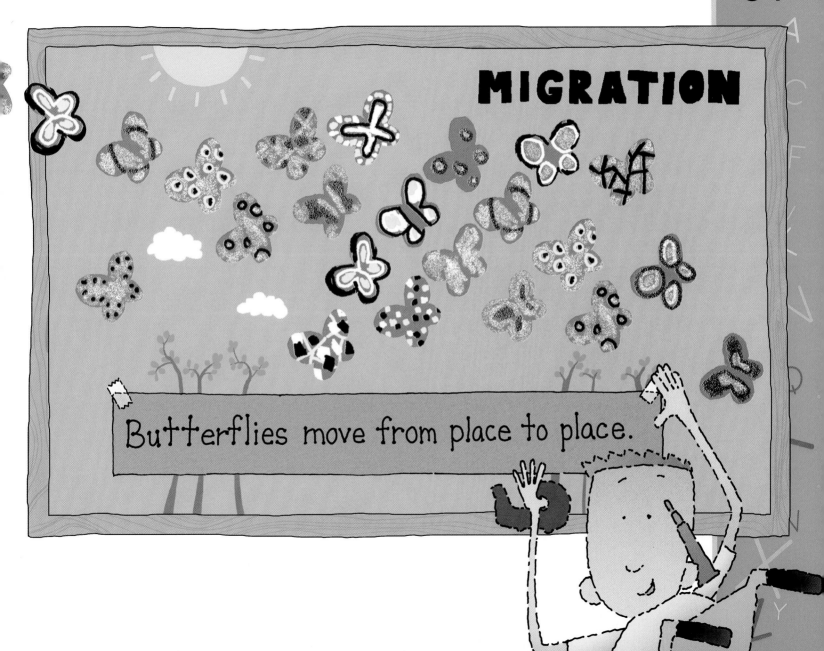

MIGRATION

Butterflies move from place to place.

Making Alphabet Books

Making an **alphabet book** is as easy as ABC. You can make one by yourself or with your class.

1 Choose a topic.

2 List words about the topic.

Words About Our School

A	art	G	gym
B	bus	H	heart
C	calendar	I	ice cream
D	dancing	J	jokes
E	Eastview	K	kindness
F	friends	L	lunch

H

H is for heart.
Your heart keeps you
alive. There are
good hearts in
this school.

♥   by Adam

F

G
G
We ha
on Tue
and it
gym f

3 Make a
page for
each letter.

4 Put the pages
together
in a book.

ABC'S
of
Eastview
School

A
B
C
D
E
F
G
H
I
J
K
L
M
N
O
P
Q
R
S
T
U
V
W
X
Y
Z

Writing About Books

Reading books is fun. Writing about books is fun, too. You can write a poem, make a poster, or tell about books in other ways.

Write a poem.

Book _Three Ducks Went Wandering_

by _Ron Roy_

One sunny day
the ducks ran away.
They wanted to play.

Make a poster.

READ
Sheep Out to Eat
by Nancy Shaw

It's very funny.
The sheep like green
food the best.

Telling About Books

Do a retelling.
- Tell important parts and favorite parts.

Do a dramatic reading.
- Read favorite parts and funny parts.

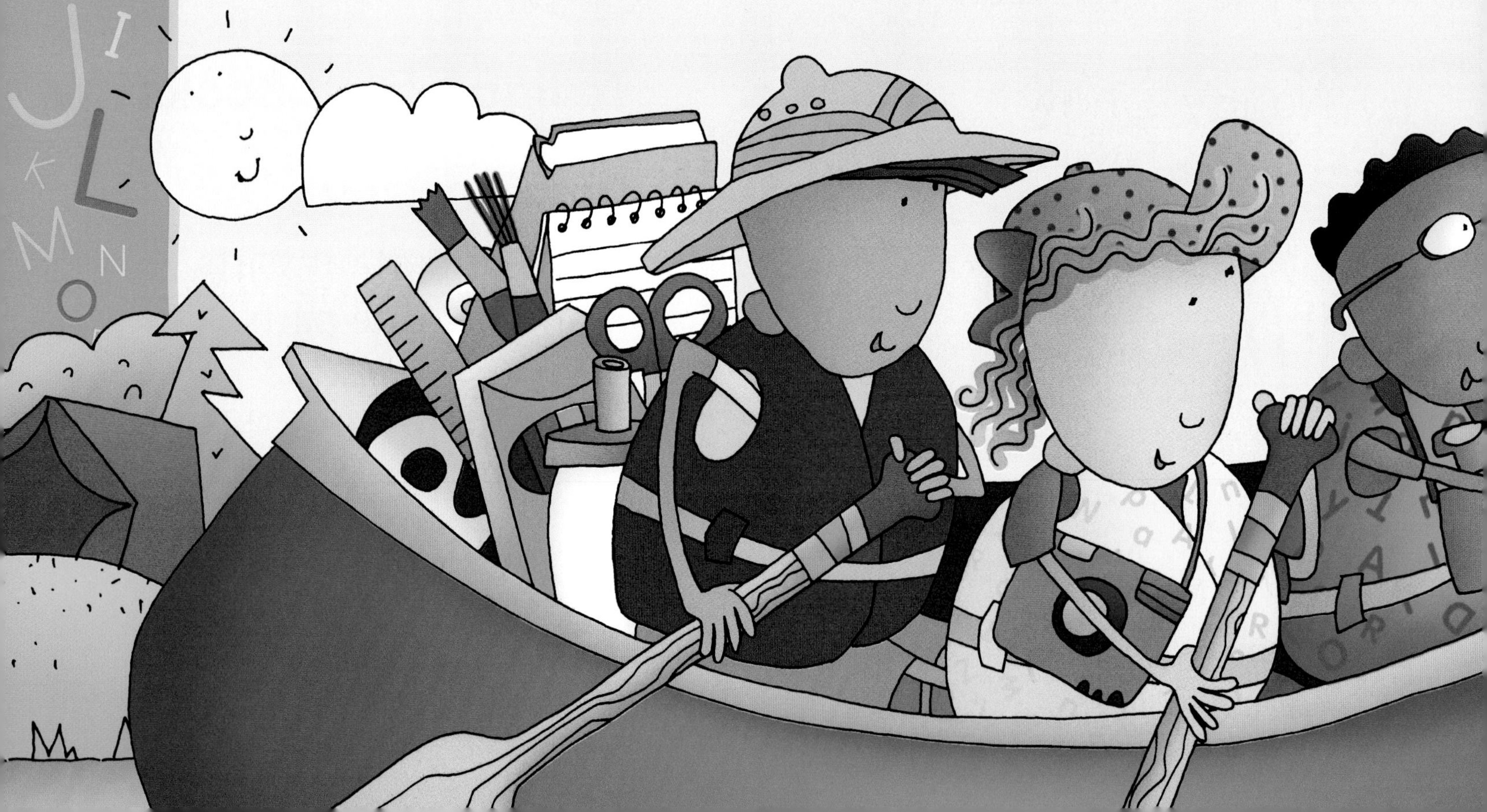

Research Writing

When you do research, you find new ideas and amazing facts. It's exciting to write and share these ideas with others.

Writing Reports

When you learn a lot about a subject, you can write about it in a **report**.

1

PLAN

- Learn about your topic.
- List or cluster the important facts.

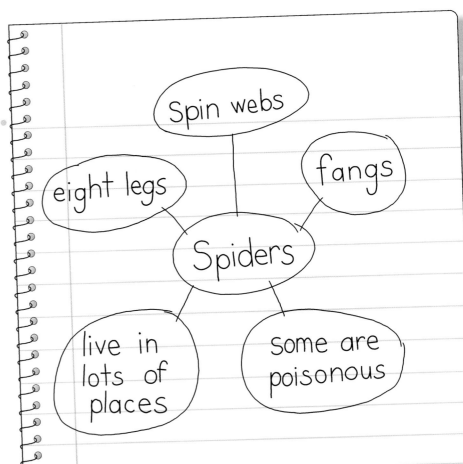

2

WRITE

- Use your list or cluster to help you write.
- Write sentences about the topic.
- Spell words the best you can.

Spiders have eight legs. Spiders have fangs. Some spiders are poisonous. Spiders spin webs. Some spiders live undrgrowd. Did you know that spiders aren't insects.

3

REVISE

- Read it aloud.
- Does it sound right?
- Make changes.

4

CHECK

- Capitals
- Punctuation
- Spelling

Spiders have eight legs.
Spiders have ^two fangs. Some
spiders are poisonous.
^Most Spiders spin webs. Some
spiders live ~~undrgrowd~~ underground.
Did you know that
spiders aren't insects~~.~~?

5

PUBLISH

- Make a neat copy.
- Share it with others.
- Put it in a class book.

April 21

Spiders

Spiders have eight legs. Spiders have two fangs. Some spiders are poisonous. Most spiders spin webs. Some spiders live underground. Did you know that spiders aren't insects?

by Todd

Writing in Learning Logs

You can write about your school work in a **learning log**. You can write facts, ask questions, and list new words.

Science Learning Log

Day 1
Today we put seeds in dirt. We put water on top. We hope a plant will grow.

Day 2
The dirt looks black. It smells like outside.

Day 5
A little plant is popping out. Ms. Hill read us a plant book. Plants need sun, air, and water.

Day

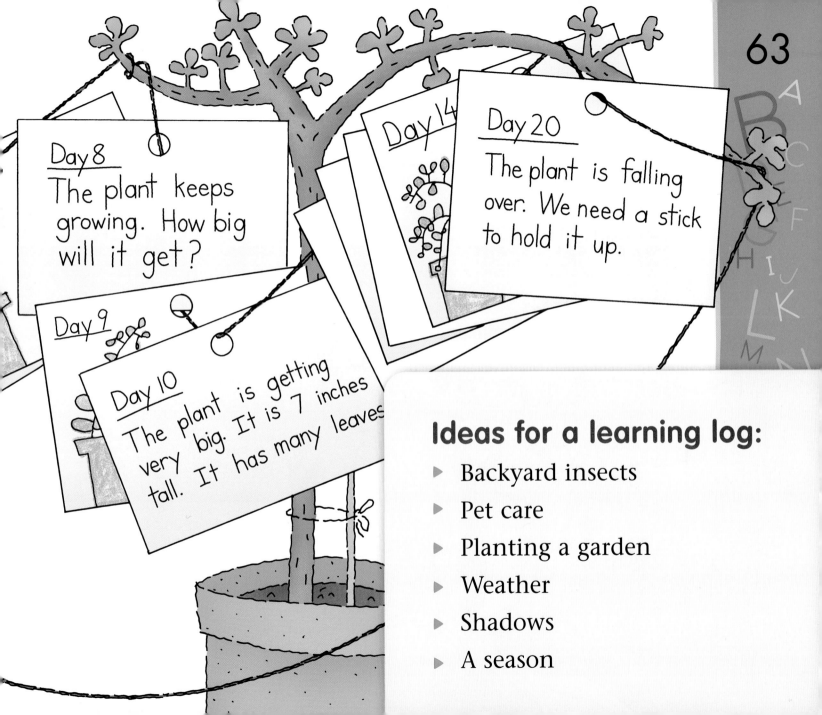

Day 8
The plant keeps growing. How big will it get?

Day 9

Day 10
The plant is getting very big. It is 7 inches tall. It has many leaves.

Day 14

Day 20
The plant is falling over. We need a stick to hold it up.

Ideas for a learning log:

▶ Backyard insects
▶ Pet care
▶ Planting a garden
▶ Weather
▶ Shadows
▶ A season

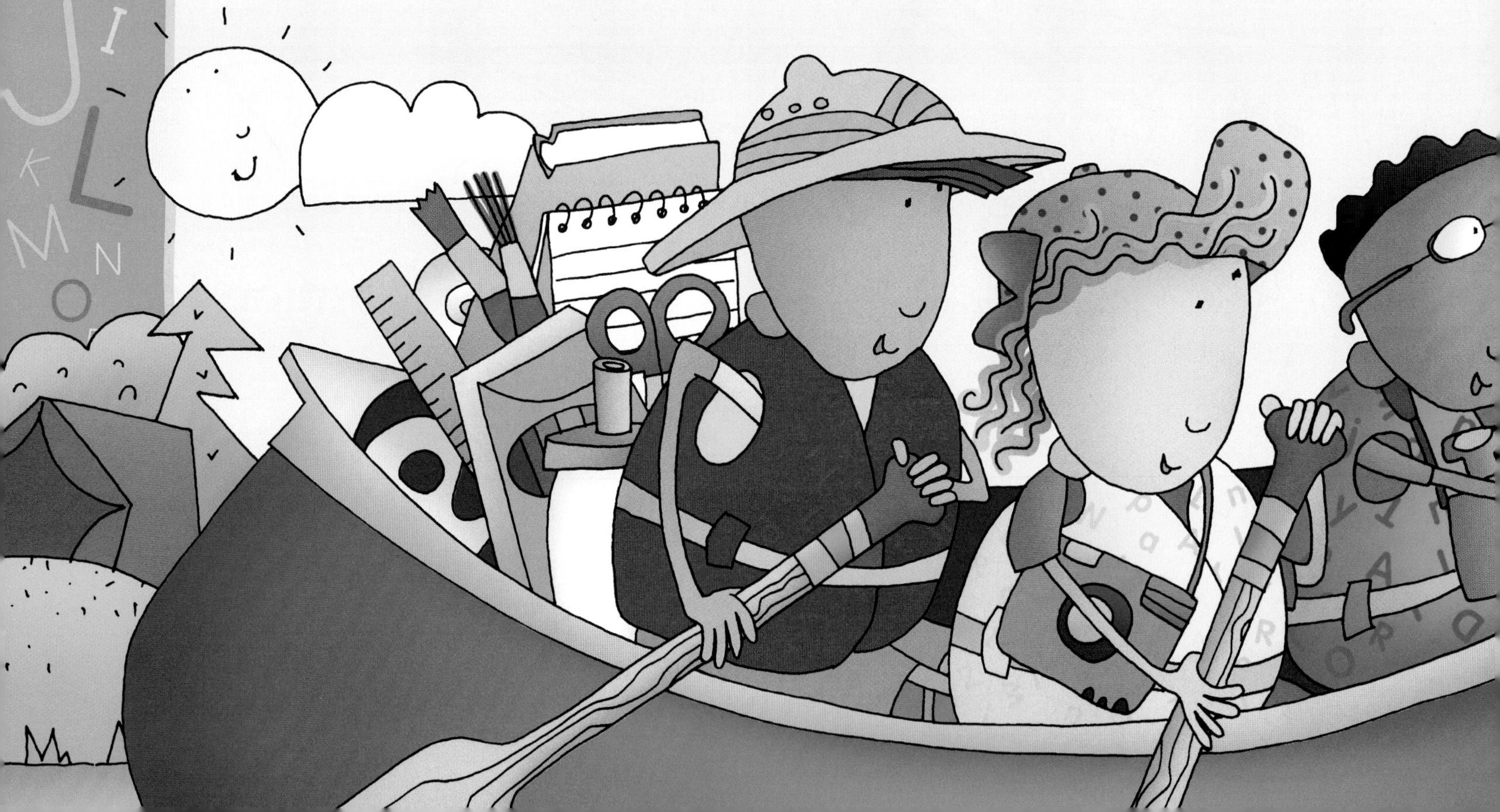

Story and Poetry Writing

Do you like to listen to stories and poems? This section will help you write stories and poems of your own. Have fun!

Writing Stories

With a little planning, writing a made-up story is easy—and a lot of fun!

You can **plan** a story with words.

- Name the characters.
- Tell what happens.

You can **plan** a story with pictures.

- Show what happens with pictures you draw or collect.

Name   Jake

Story Plan

Plan your story on this page.

Here are my characters:

Pumpkin

turtle

characters.

After Jake planned his story, he wrote it down. His story has good order.

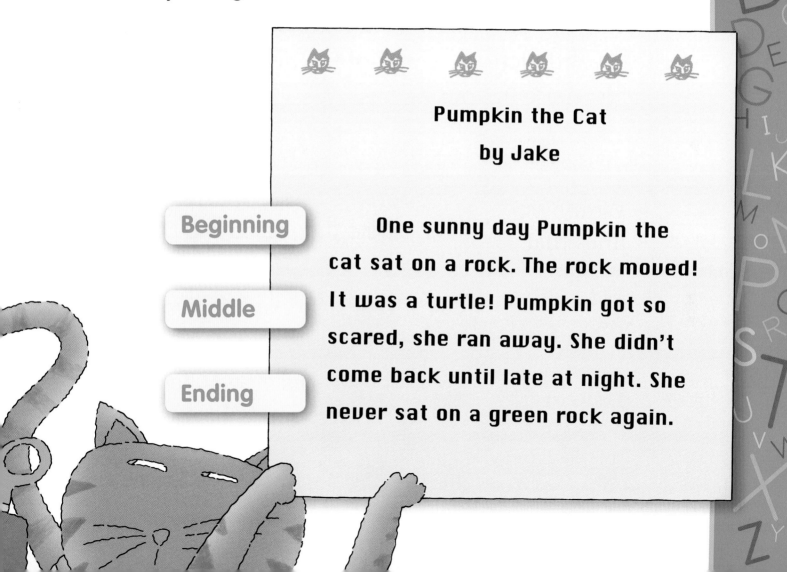

Pumpkin the Cat

by Jake

Beginning

Middle

Ending

One sunny day Pumpkin the cat sat on a rock. The rock moved! It was a turtle! Pumpkin got so scared, she ran away. She didn't come back until late at night. She never sat on a green rock again.

Writing Poems

Writing poems is like making little word pictures. Think of the best words to use in your poems.

Couplet

- Write **two** lines that rhyme.

> Sometimes comets in space
> Look like they're having a race.
> – Max

Triplet

- Write **three** lines that rhyme.

> Colors, colors everywhere,
> Colors here and colors there,
> Colors on the shirt I wear.
> – Shiere

Quatrain

- Write **four** lines.
  Make at least two lines rhyme.

Polka dots, polka dots
On my dress.
How many polka dots?
Can you guess?

– Kathleen

The owl in the tree was talking to me.
I heard him say, "Good night."
My sister says that owls don't talk.
But I know she's not right.

– Shavonn

More Poem Ideas

Tongue Twister

- Begin most of the words with the **same sound**.

> Jackson jumped and jiggled, just like a jumping jack.

Cinquain

- Write **five** lines. Use the form below.

One word (the topic)
Two words
Three words
Four words
One word

> Shadow
> Tall, short,
> Hops, waves, jumps.
> Follows where I go.
> Me!

List Poem

- Make a **list**. Here are three list poems.

Joker
On the bus
Silly
Eats cold pizza.

A name and describing words

Ideas

Snow is everywhere.
　Snow is on our school.
　Snow is on the swings.
　Snow is on the trees.
　Snow is on the houses.
　Snow is under our feet.
　Snow is on our noses.
Snow is everywhere!

　　– Clarendon School
　　　Room 36

ABC's

Aunt
Bonnie
Can
Dance
Every
Friday

Writing with Patterns

Many songs, poems, and stories follow a pattern.
Most patterns have rhyming words and a special beat.

Pattern in a Song

Once you learn
the pattern, write
your own words.

The Itsy Bitsy Spider

The itsy bitsy spider
went up the **waterspout**.
Down came the rain
and washed the spider **out**.

Out came the sun
and dried up all the rain.
Then the itsy bitsy spider
went up the spout again.

Pattern in a NEW Song

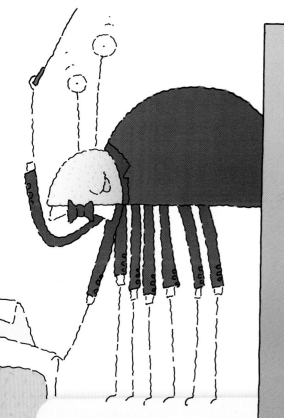

The Friendly, Funny Lobster

The friendly, funny lobster
climbed out of the blue sea.
He crawled across the sand
and sat down next to me.

He reached out a claw
and then shook hands with me.
Then the friendly, funny lobster
crept back into the sea.

More patterns:

- The Gingerbread Man
- Over in the Meadow
- This Old Man
- Miss Mary Mack

The **Tools** of Learning

Listening and Speaking Skills

This section gives you tips about being a good reader. Being a good reader can help you be a good writer, too.

Listening to Others

You can listen to your parents and your friends. You can listen to reporters on television and teachers in school. Listening is fun. It is also a great way to learn new things.

Being a Good Listener

- **BE QUIET.**
- **LOOK** at the person who is speaking.
- **LISTEN** for important words.
- **ASK** questions after the person stops talking.

Speaking to Others

Do you have something special to share?
Did you get a new toy, read a good book, or find
an interesting rock? You can show it to your
classmates. You can tell them about it, too.

Show-and-Share Tips

- **SHOW** what you are going to talk about.
- **LOOK** at your classmates.
- **SPEAK** loudly and slowly.
- **MAKE SURE** everyone can see what you are showing.
- **SHARE** important details.
- **END** with one last interesting idea.

Working Together

It's fun to do things together. You can play games, be on a team, or work in a group. Everyone in the group needs to be polite and take turns. When you work together, you can get things done. You can have fun, too.

Teamwork Tips

- **TAKE TURNS**—one person talks at a time.
- **LOOK** at the person who is speaking.
- **LISTEN** to what others have to say.
- **SHARE** your ideas, too.
- **USE** polite words as you work together.

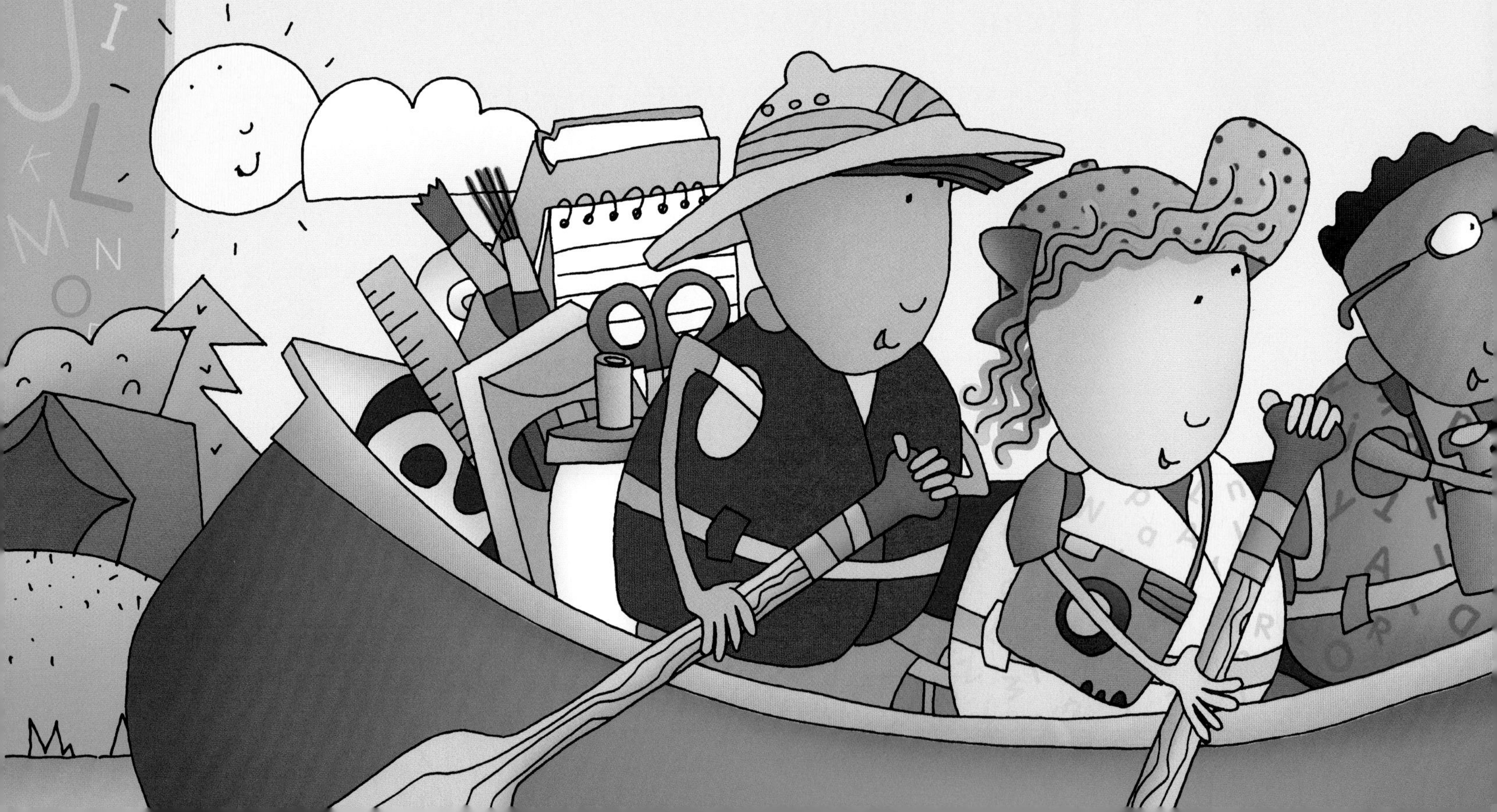

Reading and Word-Study Skills

Knowing letter names and sounds helps you with your reading. It helps you with your spelling, too.

Reading to Understand

Reading takes lots of thinking. You should think before, during, and after reading.

Think **Before** Reading

LOOK over your reading.

- Check the title.
- Look at the pictures.

PREDICT what will be in the reading.

Think **During** Reading

TRY to picture what you are reading about.

CHECK to see if your predictions are right or wrong.

Think **After** Reading

TELL yourself or someone else what the reading was about.

ASK for help if you didn't understand part of the reading.

Reading New Words

There are many ways to read new words.

Try these tips for reading new words.

LISTEN for sounds.

- Say the word slowly and listen for sounds at the beginning, middle, and end.

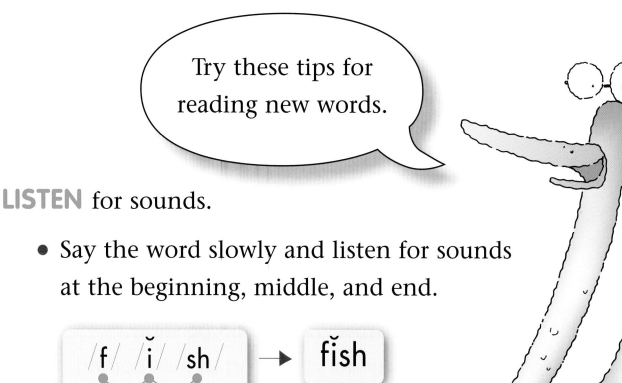

/f/ /ĭ/ /sh/ → fĭsh

LOOK for parts or patterns you know.

- If you can read but, you can read butter and button.

- If you can read hill, you can read will.

- If you can read play, you can read playing.

LOOK and **THINK**.

- Read the whole sentence.

- Ask yourself what word would make sense in the sentence.

- Look at the pictures on the page.

ASK for help.

Consonant Blends

Consonant blends are two or more consonants that come together and keep their own sounds.

fr • pr • dr	**fr**iends **pr**etty **dr**ess
bl • cl • fl	**bl**ue **cl**oud **fl**ag
sp • st • sn	**sp**ot **st**ep **sn**ow

Blends at the end of words:

de**sk** be**st** pi**nk**

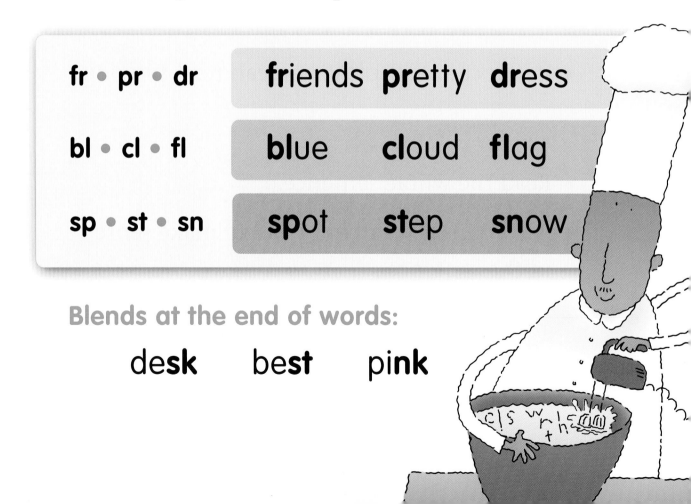

Consonant Digraphs

Consonant digraphs are two consonants that come together and make one sound.

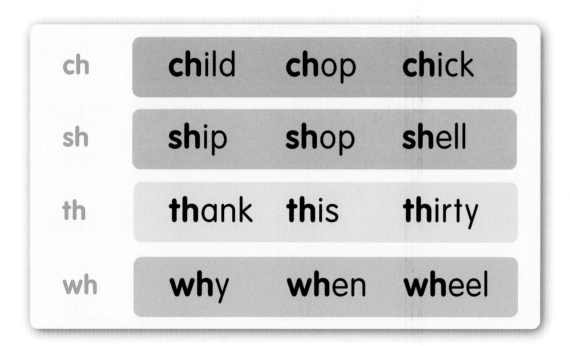

ch	child	chop	chick
sh	ship	shop	shell
th	thank	this	thirty
wh	why	when	wheel

Digraphs at the end of words:

cat**ch**   wi**sh**   ma**th**

Long Vowels

Here are two patterns for long vowel words:

consonant – vowel – consonant + e ➜ cāke

long a	long e	long i	long o	long u
tape	Pete	bike	rope	mule

consonant – vowel – vowel – consonant ➜ sōap

long a	long e	long i	long o	long u
rain	leaf	pies	boat	suit

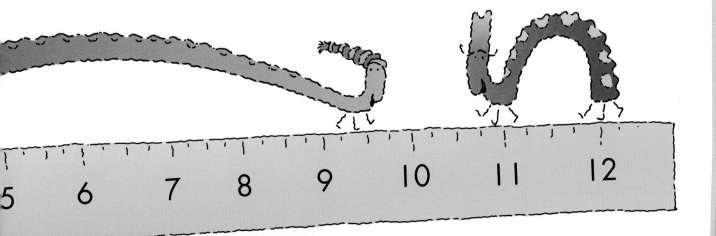

Short Vowels

Most short vowel words have this pattern:

consonant – **v**owel – **c**onsonant ➜ **sŭn**

short a	short e	short i	short o	short u
m**a**p	b**e**ll	p**i**n	h**o**p	b**u**g

5   6   7   8   9   10   11   12

Rhyming Families

Rhyming helps you read and write new words.

If you know these words, you can read and write these.

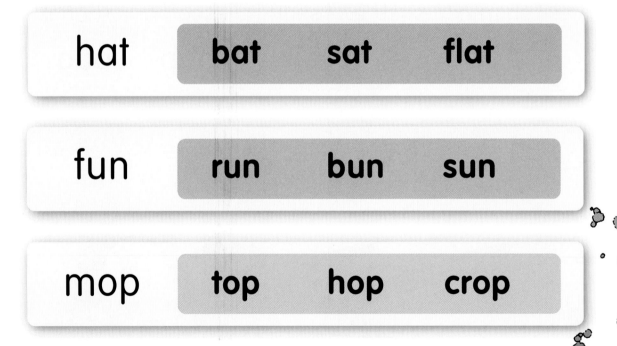

| hat | bat | sat | flat |

| fun | run | bun | sun |

| mop | top | hop | crop |

If you know these words, you can read and write these.

| fish | **wish** | **dish** | **swish** |

| cake | **lake** | **bake** | **snake** |

| like | **bike** | **hike** | **Mike** |

| rain | **pain** | **train** | **grain** |

A B C D E F G H I J K L M N O P Q R S T U V W X Y Z

Contractions

A **contraction** is one shorter word made from two words. You leave some letters out.

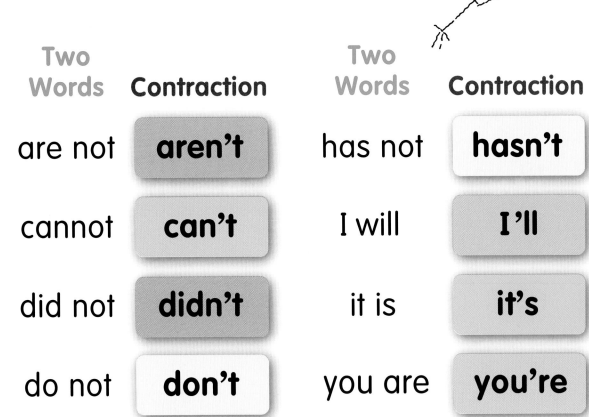

Two Words	Contraction	Two Words	Contraction
are not	**aren't**	has not	**hasn't**
cannot	**can't**	I will	**I'll**
did not	**didn't**	it is	**it's**
do not	**don't**	you are	**you're**

Compound Words

A **compound word** is a longer word made from two shorter words.

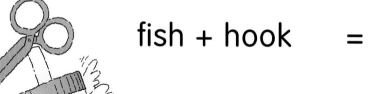

Two Words		Compound Word
base + ball	=	**baseball**
fish + hook	=	**fishhook**
pop + corn	=	**popcorn**
snow + flake	=	**snowflake**
space + ship	=	**spaceship**

Using Alphabet Lists

The alphabet can give you ideas for writing list poems and lists of words.

Alphabet List Poem

Alligator **sits,**
Butterfly **flits.**

Cup **of tea,**
Ducks **at sea.**

Eggs **to cook,**
Fish **in a brook.**

Girl named Mary,
Hat for Harry.

Igloo white,
Jacket bright.

Kite in the sky,
Ladybug shy.

Mouse near a hole,
Nest like a bowl.

Octopus below,
Penguin in the snow.

Quilt for a bed,
Rocket that's red.

Socks for running,
Turtle goes sunning.

Umbrella for showers,
Vase full of flowers.

Wagon to pull,
Box full of wool.

Yarn soft and blue,
Zipper-dee-do!

Aa

alligator

bat
map
Sam

ape

cake
play
rain

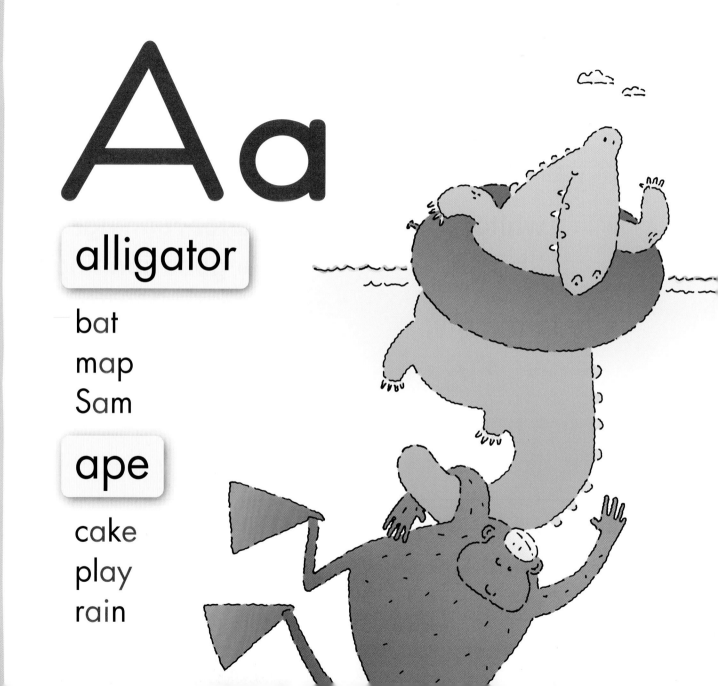

Bb

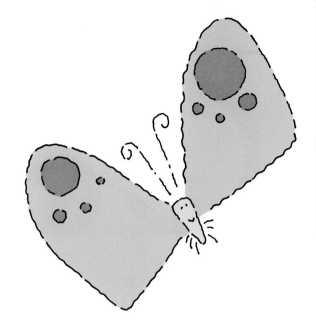

butterfly

baby
balloon
bird
book
bow
boy
bug

A
B
C
D
E
F
G
H
I
J
K
L
M
N
O
P
Q
R
S
T
U
V
W
X
Y
Z

B A
C
D E
F G
H
I
J
K L
M N
O P
Q R
S
T U
V
W
X Y
Z

Cc

cup

candle

cat

coat

cereal

cent

circle

city

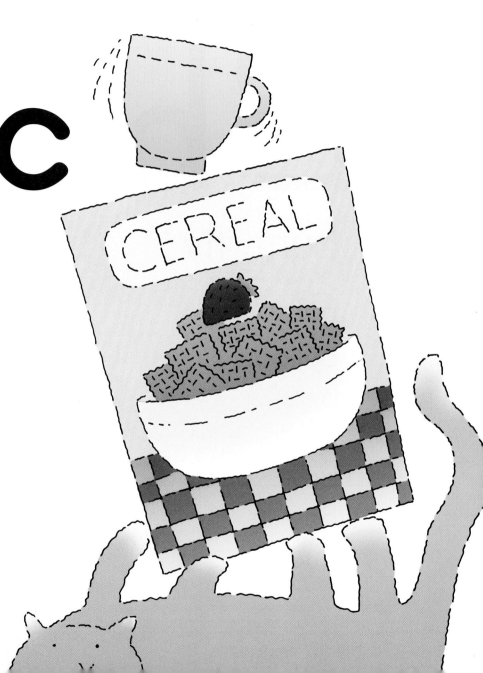

Dd

ducks

daddy
daisy
day
dinner
dinosaur
dog
door

A
B
C
D
E
F
G
H
I
J
K
L
M
N
O
P
Q
R
S
T
U
V
W
X
Y
Z

Ee

eggs

deck
Meg
pen

eagle

bean
Pete
see

Ff

fish

family
father
feet
finger
fire
food
fun

A
B
C
D
E
F
G
H
I
J
K
L
M
N
O
P
Q
R
S
T
U
V
W
X
Y
Z

Gg

girl

gate
goat
gold

gem

gerbil
giant
giraffe

Hh

hat

hair
hand
head
home
horse
house
hug

A B C D E F G H I J K L M N O P Q R S T U V W X Y Z

B
C
D
E
F
G
H
I
J
K
M
N
O
P
Q
R
S
T
U
W
X
Y
Z

I i

igloo

bib
hill
pig

ice skate

bike
pie
white

Jj

jacket

jar
jelly
jet
job
joy
juice
jungle

A B C D E F G H I J K L M N O P Q R S T U V W X Y Z

Kk

kite

kangaroo
key
kid
king
kiss
kitchen
kitten

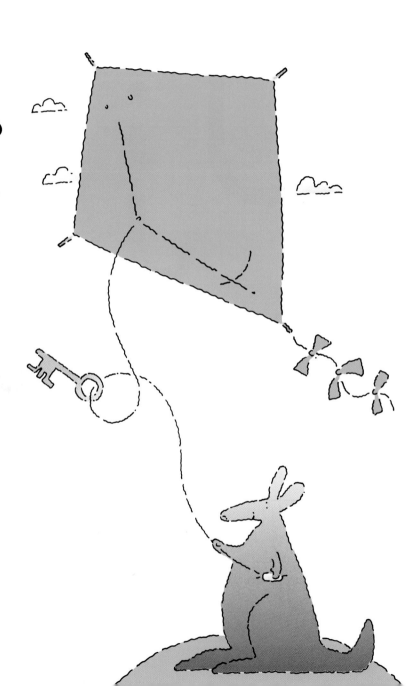

Ll

ladybug

land
laugh
leaf
leg
letter
light
love

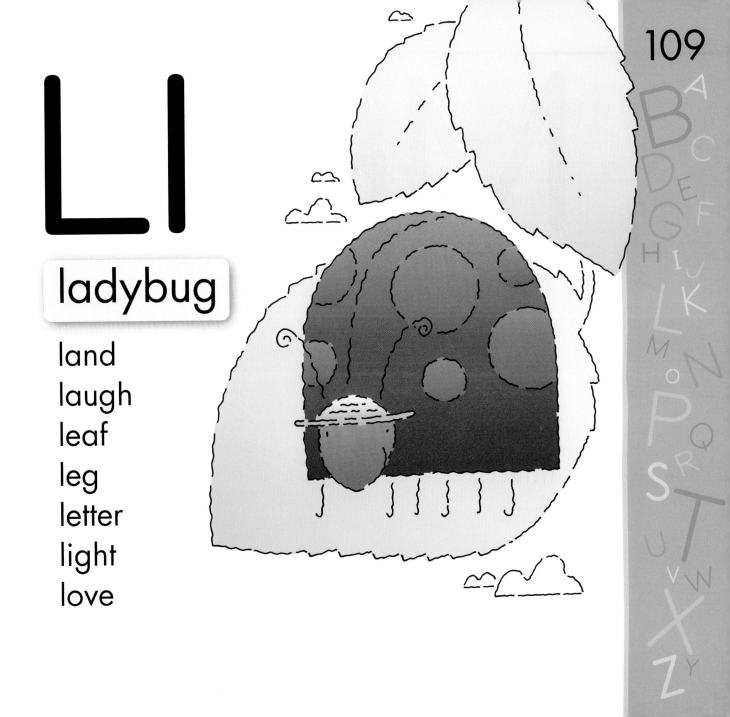

A
B
C
D
E
F
G
H
I
J
K
L
M
N
O
P
Q
R
S
T
U
V
W
X
Y
Z

B A
C
D E
F G H
I
J
K L
M N
O P
Q
S R
T U W
V
X Y
Z

Mm

mouse

mammal

man

mask

milk

moon

morning

mother

Nn

nest

name
necklace
neighbor
nickel
night
nose
nurse

A B C D E F G H I J K L M N O P Q R S T U V W X Y Z

A
B
C
D
E
F
G
H
I
J
K
L
M
N
O
P
Q
R
S
T
U
V
W
X
Y
Z

Oo

octopus

box
dog
rock

oak tree

bone
goat
no

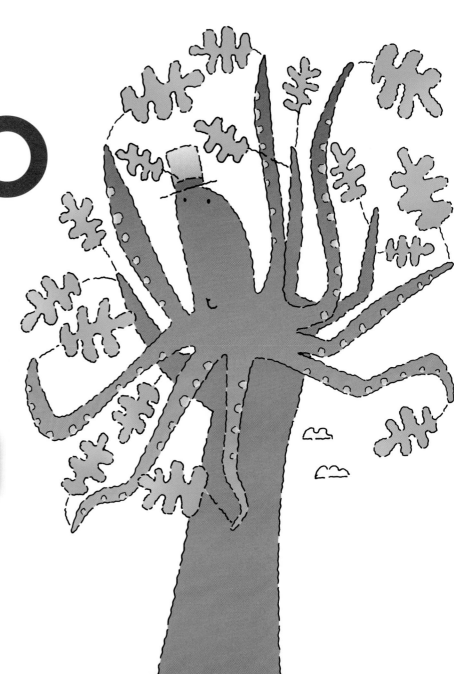

P p

penguin

paper
party
pencil
people
pet
picture
popcorn

A B C D E F G H I J K L M N O P Q R S T U V W X Y Z

Qq

quilt

quart
quarter
queen
question
question mark
quiet
quiz

Rr

rocket

rabbit
rain
rat
ring
road
room
rose

A B C D E F G H I J K L M N O P Q R S T U V W X Y Z

Ss

socks

sailboat
sand
seed
sister
soap
song
sun

T t

turtle

table
teacher
television
today
tooth
toy
turkey

A
B
C
D
E
F
G
H
I
J
K
L
M
N
O
P
Q
R
S
T
U
V
W
X
Y
Z

Uu

umbrella

duck
fun
rug

unicycle

mule
Sue
suit

Vv

vase

valentine
vegetable
vest
vine
violin
visit
voice

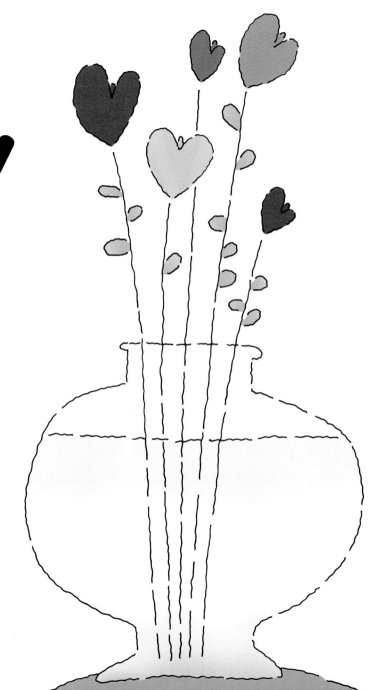

A B C D E F G H I J K L M N O P Q R S T U V W X Y Z

Ww

wagon

water
wind
window
wing
wish
wood
worm

B A
C
D
E
G H
J I
K L
M N
O P
Q R
S
T U
W V
X Y
Z

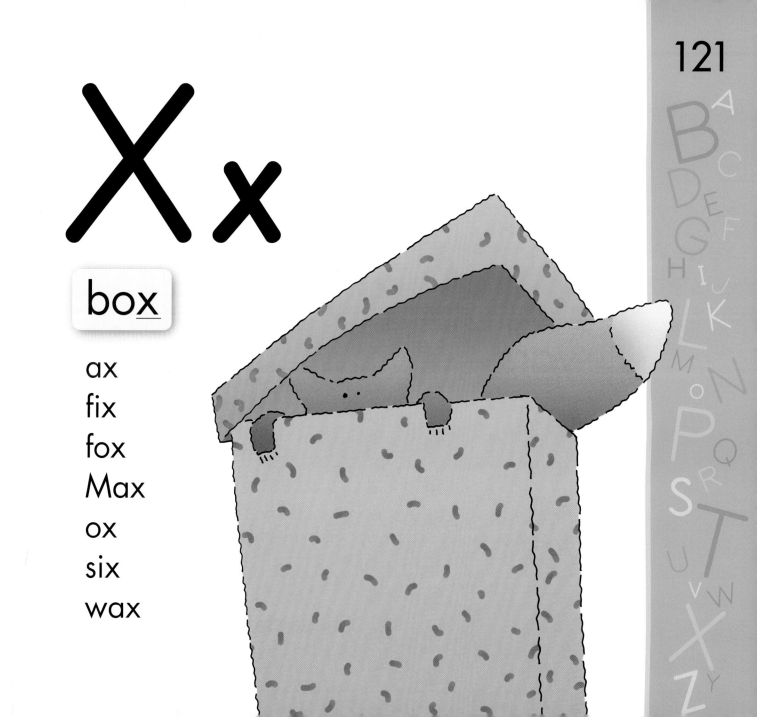

X x

bo<u>x</u>

ax
fix
fox
Max
ox
six
wax

A
B
C
D
E
F
G
H
I J K
L
M
N
O
P
Q
R
S
T
U
V W
X
Y
Z

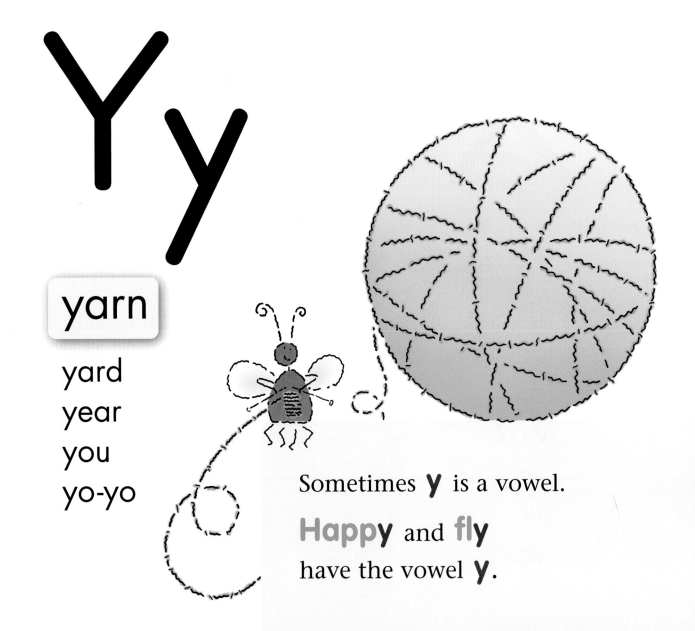

Y y

yarn

yard
year
you
yo-yo

Sometimes **y** is a vowel.
Happy and **fly**
have the vowel **y**.

B
A
C
D
E
H
G
I
J
K
L
M
N
O
P
Q
R
S
T
U
V
W
X
Y
Z

Zz

zipper

zebra

zero

zigzag

zone

zoo

zucchini

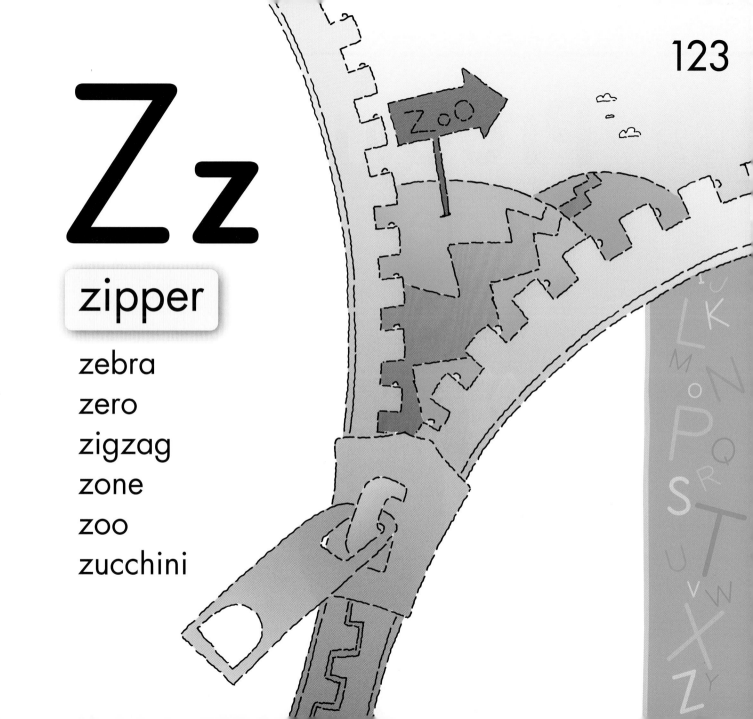

Proofreader's
Guide

Rules for Writing

All writers follow rules. In this section, you can find lots of rules to help you with your writing.

Writing Sentences

A **sentence** states a complete thought.

Mom made a big pizza.

Begin with a capital letter.

Leave a space between words.

Use end punctuation.

Kinds of Sentences

A **telling sentence** ends with a period.

> Sam ate the pizza.

An **asking sentence** ends with a question mark.

> Who is Sam**?**

An **exciting sentence** ends with an exclamation point.

> Sam is my crazy cat**!**

Using Capital Letters

You use **capital letters** in your writing.

The **first word** in a sentence

> **B**ears catch fish.

Special names

> **S**andy   **O**hio   **S**unday

The word **I**

> When can **I** go fishing?

Making Plurals

Plural means "more than one."

Add **s** for most plurals.

> friend — friend**s**

Add **es** after words ending in *s*, *x*, *ch*, and *sh*.

> glass — glass**es**   lunch — lunch**es**
>
> box — box**es**   dish — dish**es**

Change the word for a few plurals.

> child — **children**   mouse — **mice**

Using Punctuation

Use **punctuation marks** to make your writing easier to read.

Periods go after telling sentences.

> Tessa likes hats.

Periods go between dollar and cents.

> The tall hat costs $16.00.

Periods go after an abbreviation.

> Mr. Cook sells hats.

Question marks go after asking sentences.

Who is Tessa**?**

Why is she laughing**?**

Exclamation points show strong feeling.

That hat is funny**!**

Wow, it's tall**!**

Commas keep words and numbers from running together.

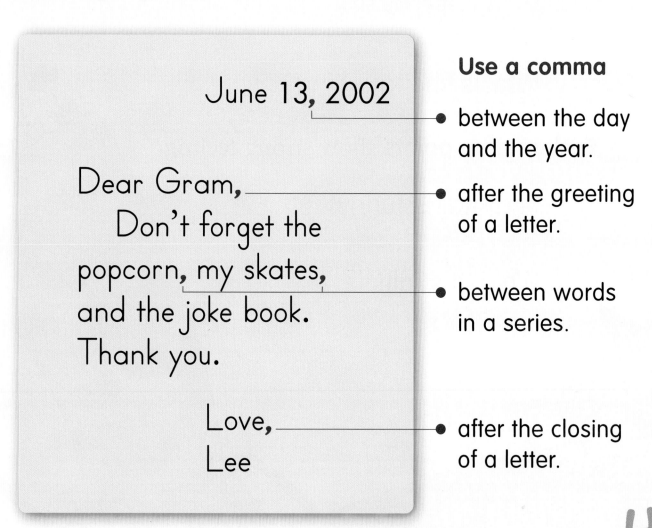

June 13, 2002

Dear Gram,
    Don't forget the popcorn, my skates, and the joke book. Thank you.

            Love,
            Lee

Use a comma

- between the day and the year.

- after the greeting of a letter.

- between words in a series.

- after the closing of a letter.

Apostrophes show ownership.

> Gram likes Lee's jokes.

Apostrophes make contractions.

> Gram can't stop laughing.

Quotation marks go around a speaker's words.

> Lee said, "Thanks for the joke book."
> "You're welcome," said Gram.

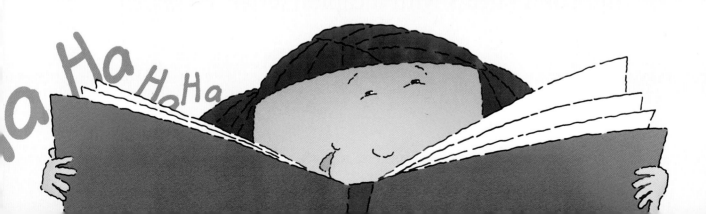

Understanding Our Language

The words we use are called the **parts of speech**.

A **noun** names a person, place, or thing.

> friend   park   apple

A **proper noun** names a special person, place, or thing and begins with a capital letter.

> Dave   Grant Park   McIntosh

A **pronoun** takes the place of a noun.

> I you he she it
> me we they them us

A **verb** shows action or helps to complete a thought.

> We **picked** lots of apples.
> The tree **was** full of red apples.

An **adjective** describes a noun or pronoun.

> Dad picked the **ripe** apples.
> I ate the **biggest** one.

B A
C
D E
F G
H I
J
K L
M
N
O P
Q
R S
T U
V
W
X
Y Z

Using Everyday Words

Everyday words are words you read and write many times a day.

A
about
after
again
all
always
am
and
any
are
ask
away

B
baby
be
because
been
before
big
book
boy
brother
but
by

C
called
can
car
children
come
could

D
did
down

E
each
eat
every

F
family
father
find
first
for
found
friend
from
funny
G get
girl
give
go
going
good

H had
happy
has
have
he
help
her
here
him
his
house
how
I if
into
is

J jump
just
K keep
knew
know
L land
last
left
let
like
little
live
long
look
love

M
- made
- make
- man
- many
- me
- more
- mother
- must
- my

N
- name
- need
- new
- next
- night
- not
- now

O
- of
- off
- old
- once
- only
- or
- other
- our
- out
- over

P
- part
- people
- place
- play
- please
- put

Q
- question

R
- ride
- right
- room
- run

S
- said
- saw
- say
- school
- she
- sister
- some
- something
- sometimes
- soon
- stop

T	**U**		
take	under	when
talk	until	where
thank	up	which
that	upon	who
the	us	why
their	use	will
them	**V** very	with
then	**W** walk	woman
there	want	won't
they	was	work
thing	way	would
this	we	write
time	well	**Y** yes
to	went	you
told	were	your
took	what	**Z** zoo

A
B
C
D
E
F
G
H I
J
K
L
M
N
O
P
Q
R
S
T
U
V W
X
Y
Z

Using the Right Word

Words that sound the same but have different meanings are called **homophones**.

ant, aunt

> A little **ant** tickled my toe.
> My **aunt** likes to dance.

ate, eight

> The rabbits **ate** the carrots.
> I saw **eight** rabbits in the garden.

blew, blue

> The wind **blew** my hair.
> The sky is **blue** on a sunny day.

for, four

> I made a card **for** Mom.
> Dad ate **four** pancakes.

hear, here

> I **hear** Ben's cat meowing outside.
> My cat is **here** beside me.

A
B
C
D
E
F
G
H
I
J
K
L
M
N
O
P
Q
R
S
T
U
V
W
X
Y
Z

knew, new

Jack **knew** Jill.
Jill has a **new** pail.

know, no

Do you **know** my name?
"**No**, I don't," said Theo.

meat, meet

The **meat** is on the grill.
We'll **meet** you at the park.

read, red

Kim **read** a poetry book.
The book has a **red** cover.

road, rode

Emma lives on that **road**.
She **rode** her bike home.

son, sun

Mr. Kitt's **son** lives in Florida.
The **sun** shines a lot in Florida.

A
B
C
D
E
F
G
H
I
J
K
L
M
N
O
P
Q
R
S
T
U
V
W
X
Y
Z

sum, some

> The **sum** of 2 + 2 is 4.
> Do you want **some** grapes?

tail, tale

> A beaver has a flat **tail**.
> Sometimes a story is called a **tale**.

to, two, too

> Let's go **to** the movies.
> I'll buy **two** tickets.
> Can we have popcorn, **too**?

won, one

Brady **won** a gold medal.
He has a silver **one** already.

wood, would

One pig had a house of **wood**.
Bub **would** like an ice-cream cone.

wear, where

May I **wear** my new shoes?
Where are my old shoes?

Student
Almanac

Lists, Maps, and Theme Words

You'll love using these pages. They have helpful information, pictures, and word lists that you can use and enjoy.

Practicing Handwriting

Neat handwriting helps you and others to read and enjoy your writing.

Handwriting Tips

- **LOOK** at handwriting models.
- **PRACTICE** letters often.
- **LEAVE** spaces between words.
- **SLANT** all letters the same way.

Manuscript Models

A B C D E F G
H I J K L M
N O P Q R S
T U V W X Y Z

a b c d e f g

h i j k l m

n o p q r s

t u v w x y z

Continuous Stroke Models

A B C D E F G
H I J K L M
N O P Q R S
T U V W X Y Z

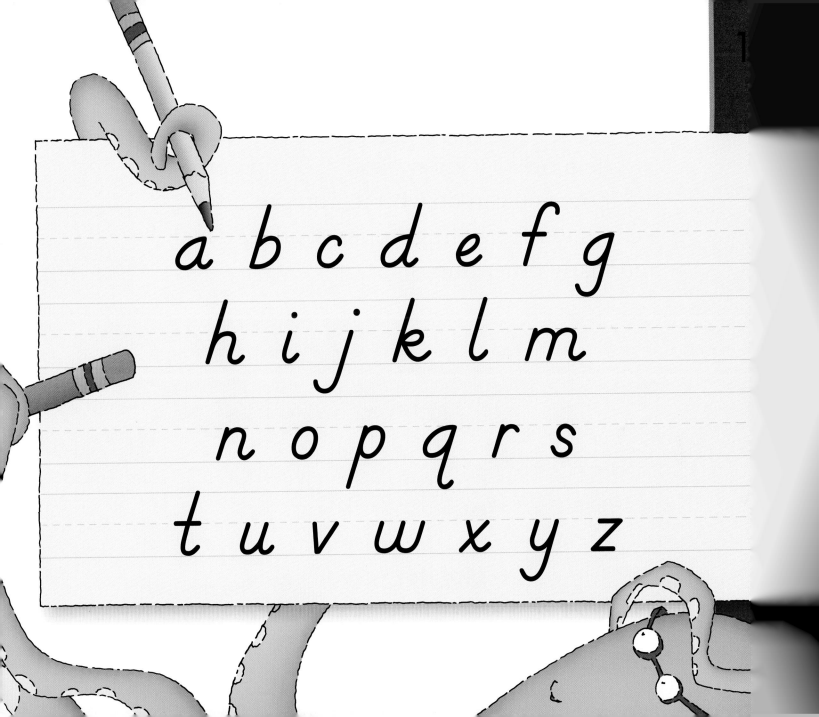

Using a Computer

The more you know about a computer, the more you can do with it. You can use a computer for writing stories, sending e-mail, and many other things.

Parts of a Computer

Computer
Disk
Keyboard
Monitor
Mouse
Printer

The mouse moves the cursor.

Using Maps

Maps help you find places near and far.

Map Signs

A **compass rose** shows directions. N is for North, E is for East, S is for South, and W is for West.

A **key** explains the symbols on a map.

United States
⭐ National Capital
–·–·– State Boundaries

Arctic Ocean

Arctic Ocean

North
America

Europe

Asia

Atlantic
Ocean

Pacific
Ocean

Africa

Equator

South
America

Indian
Ocean

Pacific
Ocean

Australia

N
W   E
S

The World
Continents and Oceans

Antarctica

A
B
C
D
E
G
H
J I
K
M
N
O
P
Q
S R
U
T V
W
X
Y

Arctic
Ocean

Alaska
(U.S.)

Greenland

N
W E
S

Canada

Pacific
Ocean

United States

Atlantic
Ocean

Mexico

Gulf of
Mexico

West Indies

North America

Central
America

South America

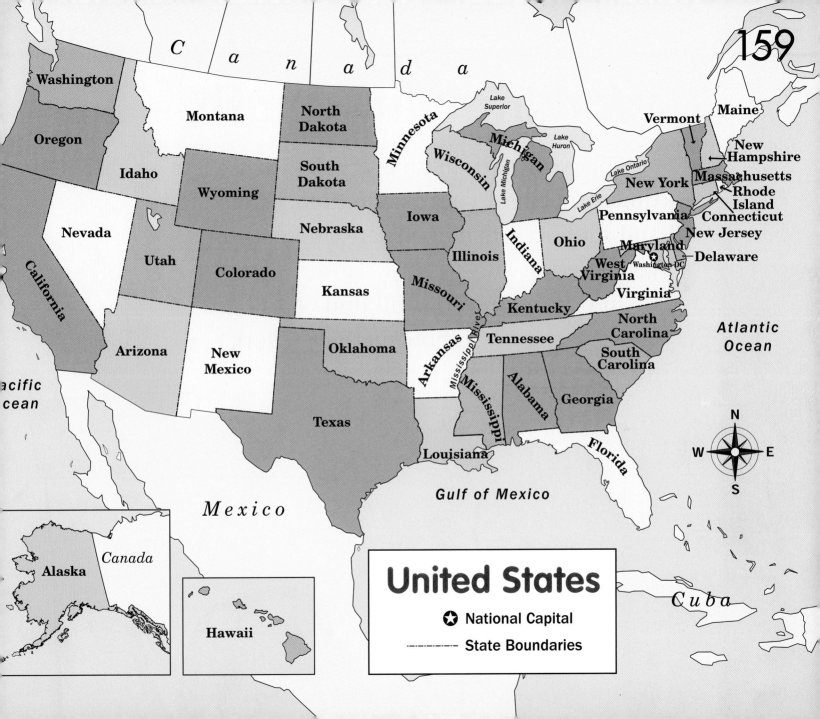

United States

⭐ National Capital

----- State Boundaries

Working with Math

You work with math every day. You tell time. You count your lunch money. You add and subtract when you share things with your friends.

In this section you will find charts and tables to show you how math can work for you.

Telling Time

Face clocks show time with hands pointing to numbers. **Digital clocks** show time with numbers. Both of these clocks show 2:30.

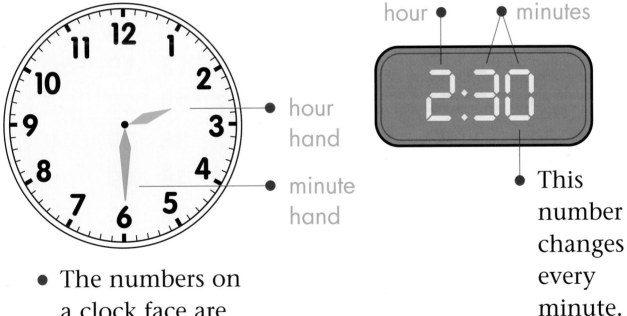

hour

minutes

hour hand

minute hand

This number changes every minute.

- The numbers on a clock face are used to tell hours and minutes.

Numbers 1 to 100

The chart below will help you count by 1's, 5's, and 10's.

Hundred Chart

1	2	3	4	5	6	7	8	9	10
11	12	13	14	15	16	17	18	19	20
21	22	23	24	25	26	27	28	29	30
31	32	33	34	35	36	37	38	39	40
41	42	43	44	45	46	47	48	49	50
51	52	53	54	55	56	57	58	59	60
61	62	63	64	65	66	67	68	69	70
71	72	73	74	75	76	77	78	79	80
81	82	83	84	85	86	87	88	89	90
91	92	93	94	95	96	97	98	99	100

Place Value

This chart shows what each part of a number is worth.

hundreds	tens	ones		
		7	=	7
	1	0	=	10
	3	2	=	32
	5	5	=	55
1	3	0	=	130

130 = **1** hundred, **3** tens, and **0** ones

Bar Graphs

A **bar graph** helps you show how many.

Children's Favorite Season

spring = 5
summer = 9
fall = 4
winter = 7

Money

 =

one dollar = four quarters

  =

one quarter = two dimes + one nickel

 =

one dime = two nickels

 =

one nickel = five pennies

Addition and Subtraction

Addition means putting numbers together.

● ● ● ●   ● ●

4 + 2 = 6

sum

- This says four plus two equals six.

Subtraction means taking numbers away.

✗✗✗✗ ● ●

6 − 4 = 2

difference

- This says six minus four equals two.

Fractions

A **fraction** is a part of something whole.

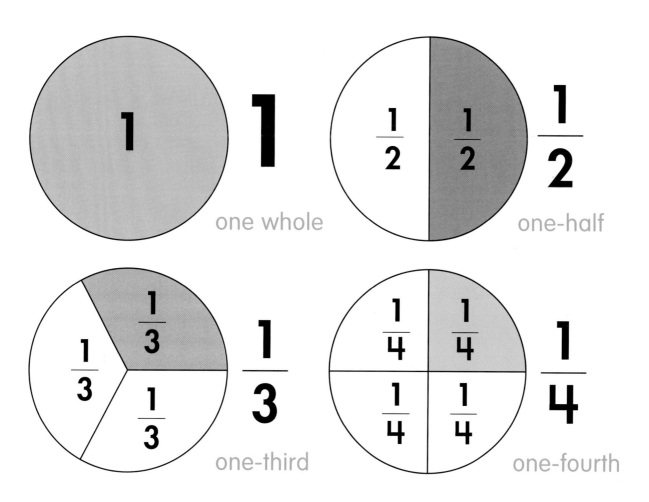

one whole   1

one-half $\frac{1}{2}$

one-third $\frac{1}{3}$

one-fourth $\frac{1}{4}$

Using Theme Words

This chapter includes word lists for important themes you will study in school.

Themes

- Days of the Week
- Months of the Year
- Seasons and Weather
- Numbers and Colors
- Places
- Parks
- Plants
- Food Pyramid
- Animals of the . . .
- Five Senses

Days of the Week

Every day brings something new.

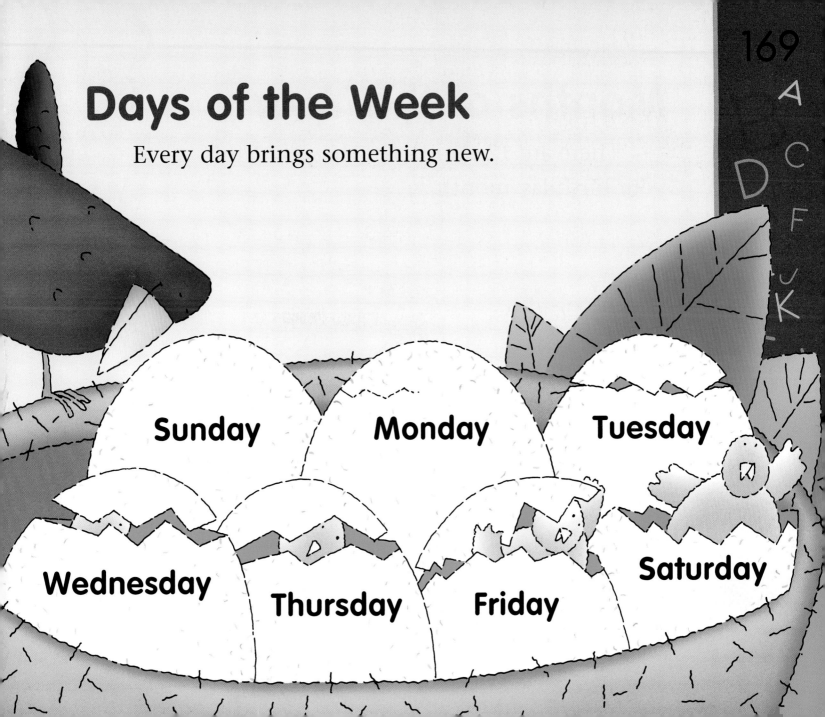

Sunday

Monday

Tuesday

Wednesday

Thursday

Friday

Saturday

Months of the Year

There are 12 months in the year. Find your birthday month.

January

February

March

July

August

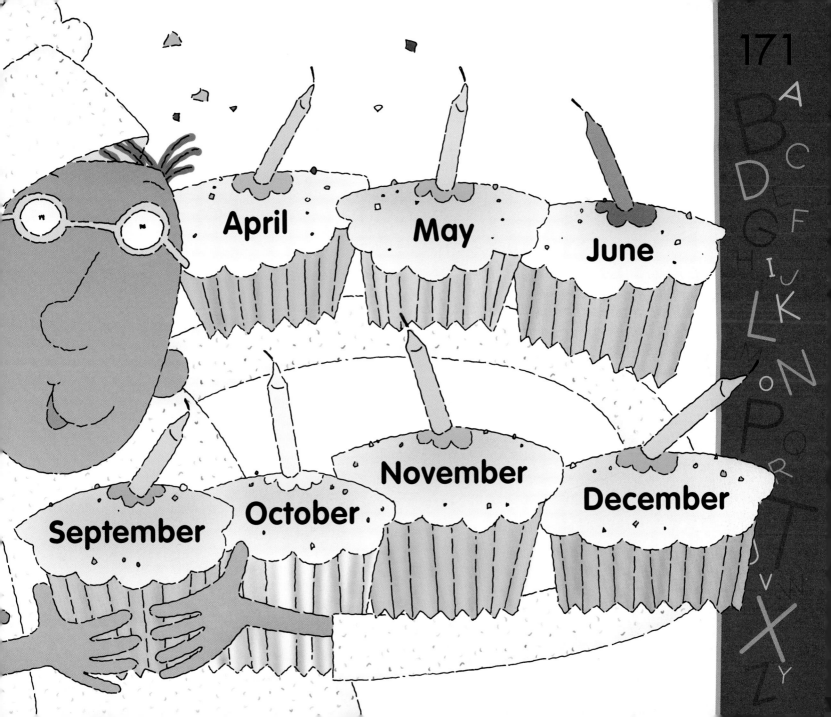

A
B
C
D
E
G
H
I
J
K
L
M
N
O
P
Q
R
S
T
U
V
W
X
Y
Z

Seasons and Weather

There are four seasons in a year. Each season has a different kind of weather. You use special words when you talk and write about the seasons and the weather.

Seasons

spring

summer

173

Weather Words

hot

rainy

partly sunny

sunny

lightning

cloudy

snowy

KABOOM
thunder

windy

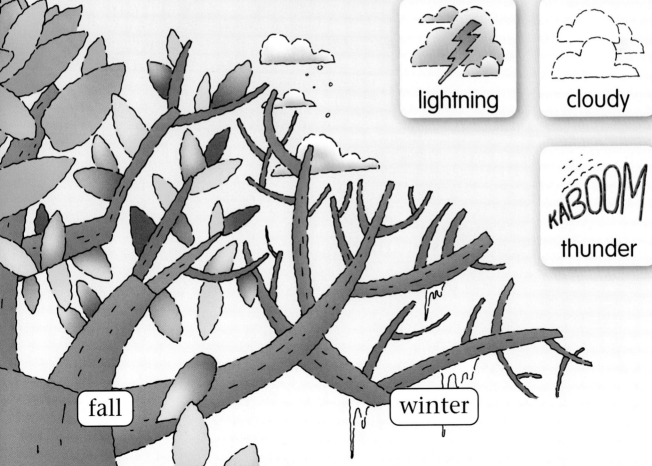
fall

winter

cold

Numbers and Colors

Numbers and colors are everywhere!

four

three

two

4

one

3

blue

2

green

yellow

zero

1

orange

0

red

A B C D E F G H I J K L M N O P Q R S T U V W X Y Z

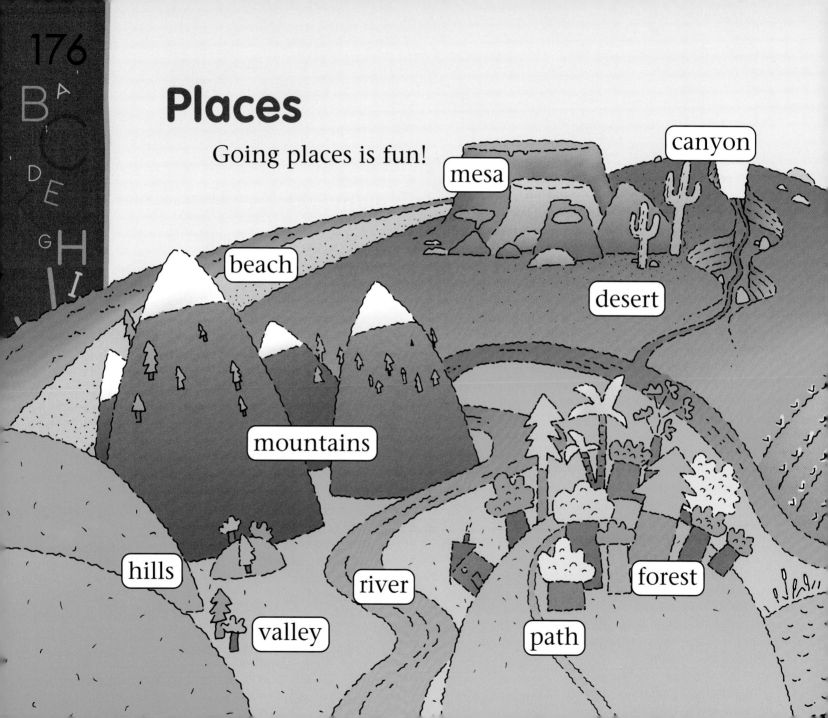

Places

Going places is fun!

canyon

mesa

beach

desert

mountains

hills

river

valley

forest

path

Parks

Parks are full of action.

run

swing

slide

ride

fly

camp

cook

read

Plants

Many kinds of plants grow on earth. Garden flowers and leafy trees are two kinds of plants. These plants need sunlight, water, air, and soil to grow. Plants make oxygen that we all breathe.

Leaves use the sunlight to make food for plants.

Roots take in water and food from the soil.

grass

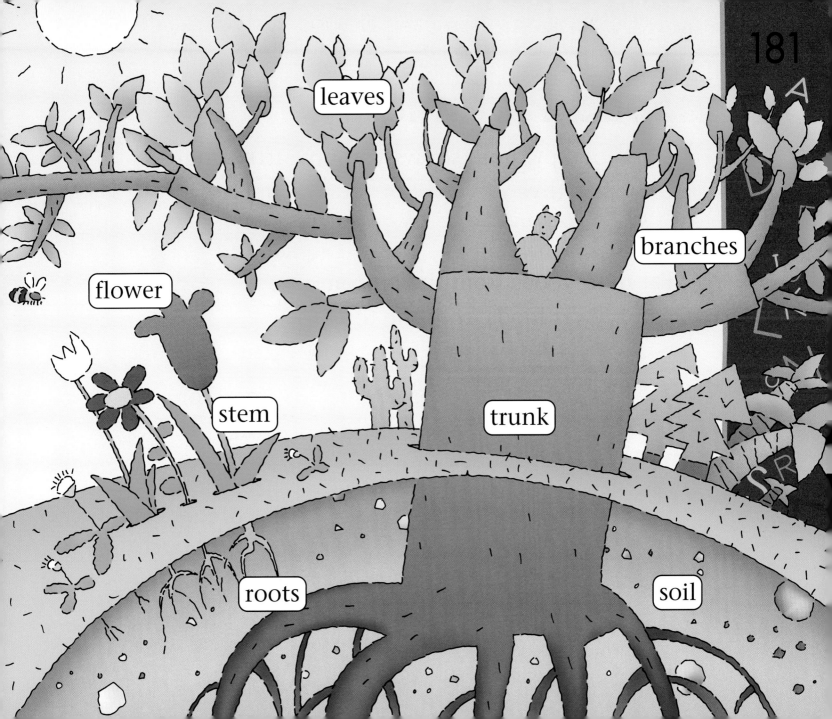

leaves

branches

flower

stem

trunk

roots

soil

Food Pyramid

A food pyramid shows you how to eat right to be healthy.

Eat more foods from the bottom and fewer foods from the top.

meat, fish, beans, eggs, nuts

fruits

bread, cereal, rice, pasta

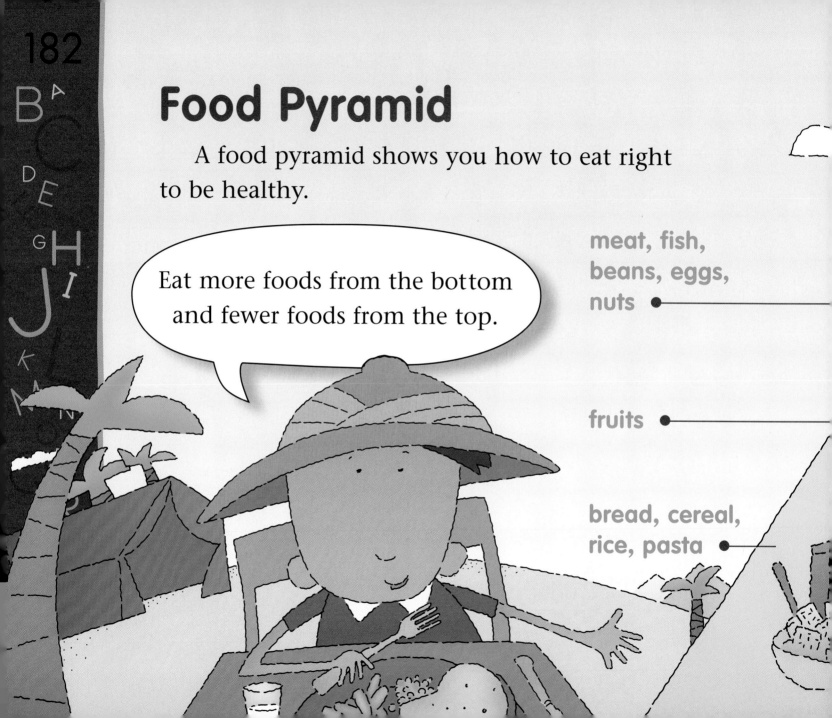

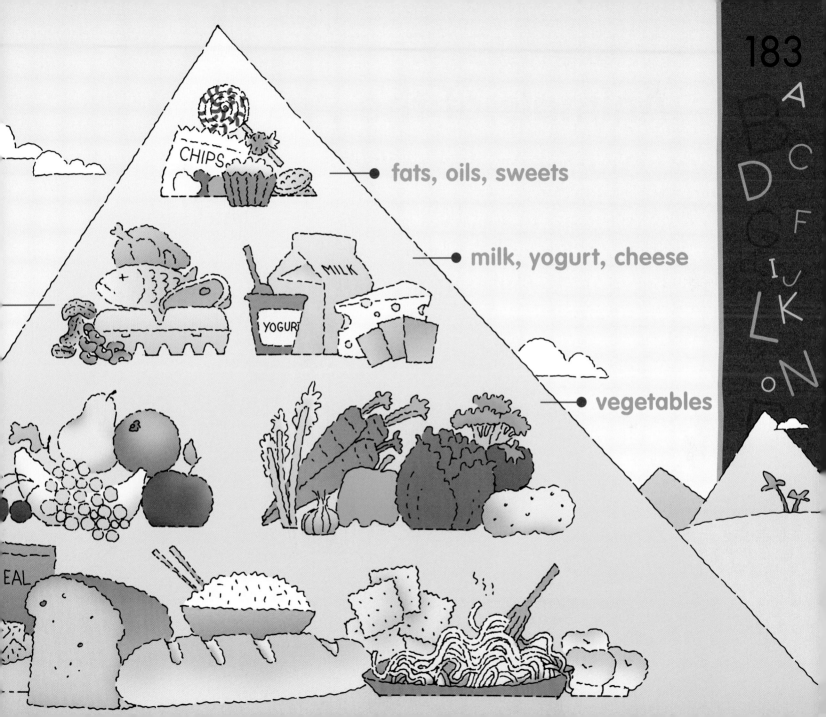

fats, oils, sweets

milk, yogurt, cheese

vegetables

CHIPS

MILK

YOGURT

EAL

B A
C O
D E
G H
I
J
K
M N
O P
Q
S R
U
V

Animals of the . . .

Oceans	Woodlands	Grasslands
crab	bear	antelope
fish	beaver	elephant
octopus	chipmunk	giraffe
shark	deer	hippopotamus
starfish	porcupine	lion
stingray	raccoon	prairie dog
whale	skunk	zebra
	squirrel	

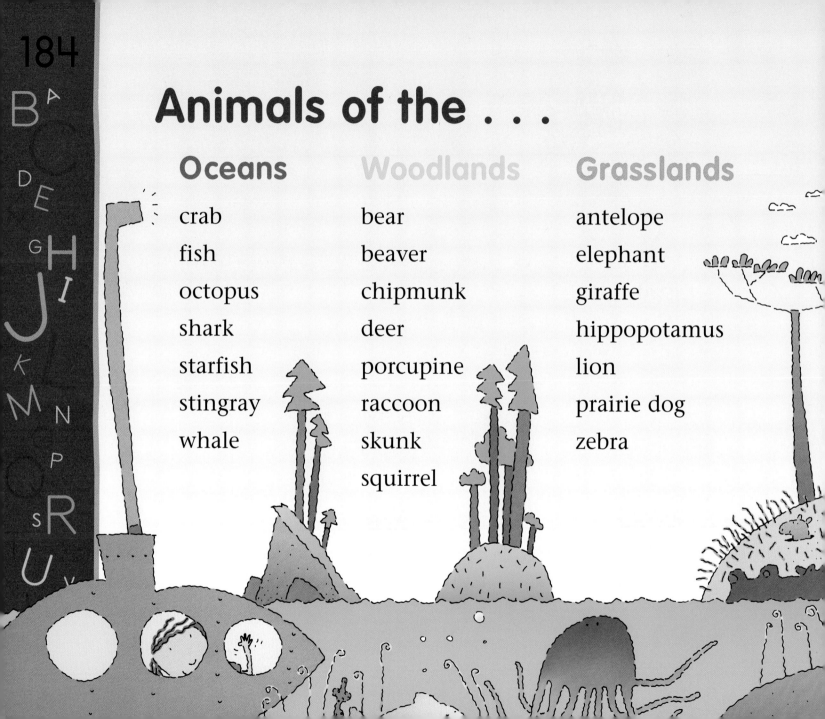

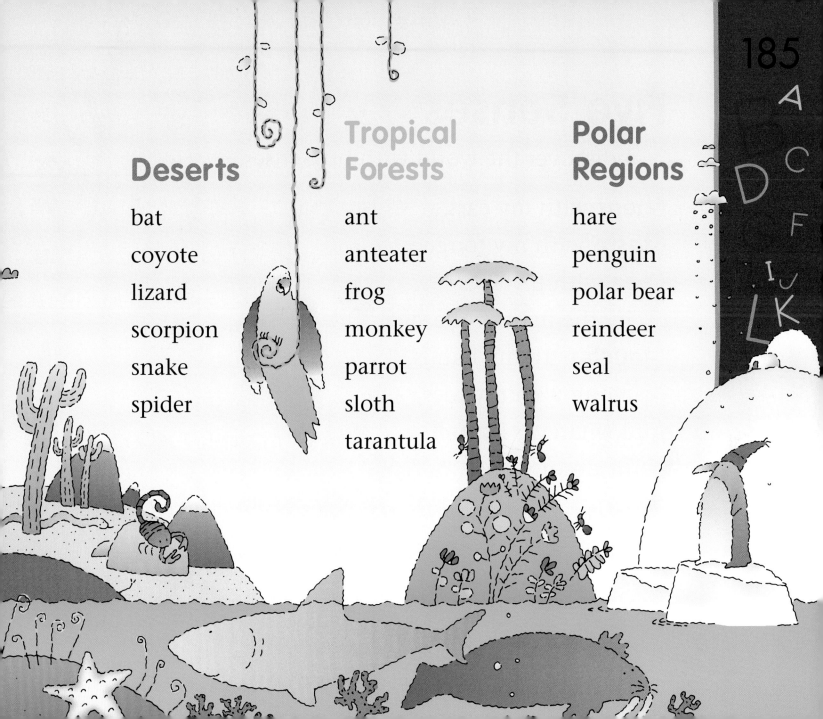

Deserts

bat
coyote
lizard
scorpion
snake
spider

Tropical Forests

ant
anteater
frog
monkey
parrot
sloth
tarantula

Polar Regions

hare
penguin
polar bear
reindeer
seal
walrus

Five Senses

I discover the world with my senses.

I **hear** with my ears,
I **taste** with my tongue,
I **see** with my eyes
by the light of the sun.
I **touch** with my hands,
along with my toes,
And whatever I **smell**
tickles my nose.